THE MUHAMMADAN DRINK

SAQIBI SEIF

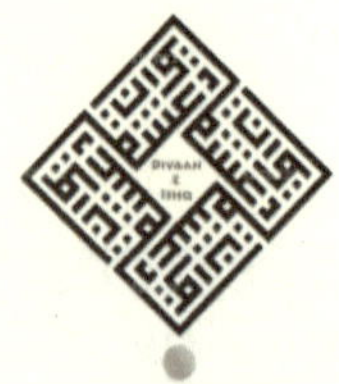

ISBN 978-1-7774584-9-2

Book Cover Art: "Ya Shafi" ("O Healer") by Sana Mirza

Sana Mirza's Website: muhammadanart.com

Connect to Saqibi Seif:

Instagram: @sourceascension

TABLE OF CONTENTS

"Do not liken Ahl al-Bayt to any other, for they merit supremacy. To hate them is mankind's utter ruin, and to love them is tremendous worship." - Ibn Arabi (qs), from the book " Al-Sharf al-Mu'abbad li Aal Muhammad S.A.W" aka "The Continuous Esteem of the Prophet's Family S.A.W" By Sheikh Yusuf al-Nabhani

DEDICATION

I dedicate this book to all lovers of **Mustafa Ahmad Muhammad** ﷺ & The People of the Cloak (Ahl al-Kisa), which is comprised of **Mustafa Ahmad Muhammad** ﷺ; his daughter, Fatimah (as); his son-in-law, Ali (as); and their children, Hasan (as) and Husayn (as). May this book be a means for us to be purified & spiritually elevated so that we may be under such a Heavenly Cloak so that we may be accepted in the Divinely Presence.

Ameen! Ameen! Ameen!

ACKNOWLEDGEMENTS

I'd like to acknowledge Alicia Ali, the one who/Hu is continuously supporting & helping me to publish my books so that we may all positively benefit from this labour of love for Haqq, Divine Truth. May Allah Almighty Bless you Eternally & beyond for all of the service that you're rendering. Ameen! Ameen! Ameen! I can never thank/reward you enough, your thanks/reward is with Allah Almighty. But ultimately I'd like to thank Allah Almighty for giving me such a willpower and inspiration to write such a book, for all goodness comes from Him alone. I'd also like to thank Him for opening up such a way for me to write what is written within these pages. But no such thankfulness can truly be worthy of thanking Him as He deserves.

Glossary of Arabic Text

ﷺ = Sallallahu Alayhi Wasallam (peace be upon him and his family)

رضي الله عنه = Radi Allah anhu (peace be upon him)

قدس الله سره = qaddas allahu sirrahu (may Allah sanctify his secret/life)

عَلَيْهِ ٱلسَّلَامُ = Alayhi As-Salaam aka "(as)" (peace be upon upon you)

"وافي زلامل ليالي كالا علي"

"Wafi Zulamil Layaali Kalla aali!"

"And I follow in the footsteps of the Holy Prophet, the Full Moon of Perfection." - Shaykh Abdul Qadir Al Jilani (qs) from the Qasida Ghousia Sharif

PREFACE

بِسْمِ اللهِ الرَّحْمٰنِ الرَّحِيْمِ

(In the Name of Allah, the most Merciful, the most Compassionate)

I've intended to write these pages & publish this book in the blessed month of Rabbi Awal, the blessed month in which **Mustafa (The Chosen One) Ahmad (Most Praise Worthy) Muhammad (Most Praised)** ﷺ was born in, with the intention of us gaining Baraka (Divine Blessing) & Shifa (Divine Cure), hence the "Ya Shafi" book cover art on this book. We are intending to get His Cure through His most beloved ones: **Mustafa Ahmad Muhammad** ﷺ, Ahl al Bayt , **his** ﷺ companions, and those that love/follow them aka the saints, peace and blessings be upon them all. Hayy Mashallah!

Each page is a sip from the eternal fountain of wine of the love from **Mustafa Ahmad Muhammad** ﷺ, drinking until nothing but **his** ﷺ purity remains within this very fragile "I" that we all grievously tend to attach ourselves with. Hayy Mashallah!

You don't purchase this wine with money, but you purchase it with your heart, and the more you give from your heart to **him** ﷺ then the more Heavenly wine you'll have in your possession. Within these pages are my tastes of the wine of Divine Love and "I" try my best to articulate such a meticulous taste when walking The Muhammadan Way. Hayy Mashallah!

Let us invigorate ourselves with each sip, let us become drunk as well as healed ones with the love that Allah Almighty deemed worthy of reflecting "Him" as "He" Willed from pre-Eternal up to Eternal. The Muhammadan Love. Hayy Mashallah!

Every sacred sip from the Muhammadan Drink will cleanse us from all impure facets of our lives, making us sincere, good, pure, and acceptable ones in the Divinely Presence. Hayy Mashallah!

Let us get lost into the endless fountain of Divine Intoxication which purifies us for the meeting with the Divinely Presence. Hayy Mashallah!

Any mistakes within these pages are from me, a weak servant of Allah Almighty. Any goodness you'll read here Is from the bountiful gaze of Allah Almighty. Hayy Mashallah! May Allah Almighty forgive us and accept this humble labour of love for **Mustafa Ahmad Muhammad** ﷺ from us. Ameen! Ameen! Ameen!

Al-Fatiha. (The first chapter in the Qur'an, "The Opener").

SALAWATS UPON MUSTAFA AHMAD MUHAMMAD ﷺ + NADI ALI (AS)

بِسْمِ اللهِ الرَّحْمٰنِ الرَّحِيْم

Transliteration: bismillāhi r-raḥmāni r-raḥīm

Translation: In the Name of Allah, the most Merciful, the most Compassionate

Salawat Al-Fatih / The Salutation of the Victor

اَللَّهُمَّ صَلِّ عَلى سَيِّدِنَا مُحَمَّدٍ اَلْفَاتِحِ لِمَا أُغْلِقَ وَ اَلْخَاتِمِ لِمَا سَبَقَ نَاصِرِ الْحَقِّ بِالْحَقِّ وَ الْهَادِي إِلى صِرَاطِكَ الْمُسْتَقِيمِ وَ عَلَى آلِهِ حَقَّ قَدْرِهِ وَ مِقْدَارِهِ الْعَظِيم

"Allahumma salli `alaa Sayyidinaa Muhammadi 'l-faatihi limaa ughliq, wa 'l-khaatimi limaa sabaq, naasiri 'l-haqqi bi 'l-haqq, wa 'l-haadi ilaa Siraatika 'l-Mustaqeem, wa `alaa aalihi haqqa qadrihi wa miqdaarihi 'l-`azheem."

"O Allah, bless our Master Muhammad, who opened what was closed and sealed what was before. He makes the truth victorious by the Truth and he is the guide to Your Straight Path. And bless his Household as it befits his immense stature and splendor." Ameen! Ameen! Ameen!

Scholars have said if you recite this once, it is as if you recited Dala`il al-Khayrat 600,000 times! Another says if you recite salawats on the number of human beings from the time of Sayyidina Adam (as) until Judgment Day, that is the value of Salaat al-Faatih!

Transliteration: "Allahuma salli ala Sayyinda Muhammadin adada hilmika wa salli ala Sayyinda Muhammadin adada ilmika wa salli ala Sayyidna Muhammadin adada kalimatika!" Ameen! Ameen! Ameen!

The Salawat above is from a section from the Dala'il al-Khayrat (The Waymarks of Benefits & Brilliant Burst of Lights in the Remembrance of Blessings on the Chosen Prophet), written by Muhammad Sulaiman al-Jazuli قدس الله سره.

Translation: "O Allah, exalt our Master Muhammad to the extent of Your Forbearance! O Allah, exalt our master Muhammad to the extent of Your Knowledge! O Allah, exalt our Master Muhammad on the number of Your Words!" Ameen! Ameen! Ameen!

NADI ALI (AS)

بِسْمِ اللّٰهِ الرَّحْمٰنِ الرَّحِيْمِ

نَادِ عَلِيًّا مَظْهَرَ الْعَجَائِبِ تَجِدْهُ عَوْنًا لَّكَ

فِي النَّوَائِبِ كُلُّ هَمٍّ وَّغَمٍّ سَيَنْجَلِيْ

بِعَظَمَتِكَ يَا اَللهُ وَبِنُبُوَّتِكَ يَا مُحَمَّدُ

وَبِوَلَايَتِكَ يَا عَلِيُّ يَا عَلِيُّ يَا عَلِيُّ

Transliteration: bismillāhi r-raḥmāni r-raḥīm

Nadi Aliyan Madh'haral Ajaaeb
Tajid'hoo Aunnallaka Fin-Nawaaib
Kullu Hammin Wa Ghammin Sayanjali
Be Azmatika Ya Allah Hu
Be Nabooatika Ya Muhammadu
Wa Be Wilaayatika Yaa Aliyyu, Yaa Aliyyu, Yaa Aliyu!

Translation: In the name of Allah, the most Merciful, the most Compassionate

Call upon Imam Ali عَلَيْهِ ٱلسَّلَامُ who manifests wondrous appearances, he will rescue and support you in times of difficulties and calamities. All grief and sorrows will disappear, By the Might of Allah, by Thy Apostleship! O Muhammad ﷺ, and by Thy Authority O Ali (as)! O Ali (as)! O Ali (as)!

DASTOOR (I ASK PERMISSION FOR YOUR) MADAD (HELP) YA (O):

Mustafa Ahmad Muhammad ﷺ,

Abu Bakr as-Siddiq رضي الله عنه,
Abu Yazid al-Bistami ‘قدس الله سره,
Khwaja Muhammad al-Maghrabi ‘قدس الله سره,
al-'Arabi Abu Yazid al-'Ishqi al-Iraqi ‘قدس الله سره,
Abul Mudhaffar at-Turk at-Tusi ‘قدس الله سره,
Abul Hasan 'Ali ibn Ja'far ibn Salman al-Kharqani ‘قدس الله سره,
Sayyid Abul Qasim al-Jurgani ‘قدس الله سره,
Abu 'Ali al-Farmadi ‘قدس الله سره,
Abu Yaqub Yusuf al-Hamadani ‘قدس الله سره,
Abul Abbas, al-Khidr ‘قدس الله سره,
'Abdul Khaliq al-Ghujdawani ‘قدس الله سره,
'Arif ar-Riwakri ‘قدس الله سره,
Khwaja Mahmud al-Anjir al-Faghnawi ‘قدس الله سره,
'Ali ar-Ramitani ‘قدس الله سره,
Muhammad Baba as-Samasi ‘قدس الله سره,
as-Sayyid Amir Kulal ‘قدس الله سره,
Khwaja Baha'uddin Bukhari Shah Naqshband ‘قدس الله سره,
'Ala'uddin al-Bukhari al-Attar ‘قدس الله سره,
Yaqub al-Charkhi ‘قدس الله سره,
Ubaydullah al-Ahrar ‘قدس الله سره,
Muhammad az-Zahid ‘قدس الله سره,
Darwish Muhammad ‘قدس الله سره,
Muhammad Khwaja al-Amkanaki ‘قدس الله سرهه,
Muhammad al-Baqi bi-l-Lah ‘قدس الله سره,
Ahmad as-Sirhindi ‘قدس الله سره,

Muhammad al-Masum ‘قدس الله سره,
Muhammad Sayfuddin al-Mujaddidi ‘قدس الله سره,
as-Sayyid Nur Muhammad al-Badawani ‘قدس الله سره,
Mirzā Mazhar Jān-i Jānān Shamsuddin Habib Allah ‘قدس الله سره,
Shah Ghluam ‘Ali ‘Abdullah ad-Dahlawi ‘قدس الله سره,
Mawlana Khalid al-Baghdadi ‘قدس الله سره,
Shaykh Ismail Muhammad ash-Shirwani ‘قدس الله سره,
Khas Muhammad Shirwani ‘قدس الله سره,
Muhammad Effendi al-Yaraghi ‘قدس الله سره,
Jamaluddin al-Ghumuqi al-Husayni ‘قدس الله سره,
Abu Ahmad as-Sughuri ‘قدس الله سره,
Abu Muhammad al-Madani ‘قدس الله سره,
as-Sayyid Sharafuddin ad-Daghestani ‘قدس الله سره,
Mawlana ‘Abdullah al-Fa’iz ad-Daghestani ‘قدس الله سره,
Mawlana Shaykh Nazim Adil al-Qubrusi ‘قدس الله سره,
Mawlana Shayh Mehmet Adil Al-Rabbani ‘قدس الله سره,
Mawlana Amir al-Muminin Shah e-Mardan Imam ‘Ali b. Abi Talib wa Saheb uz-Zaman Imam Muhammad al-Mahdi al-Muntadhar’alaihi salam عَلَيْهِ ٱلسَّلَامُ

“Lo! Allah preferred Adam and Noah, the Family of Abraham, and the Family of Imran above all other beings, They were descendants of one another. Allah is Hearer, Knower.” –Al-Qur’an from Surah Ali Imran (3:33)

“Narrated by Abdullah b. Abbas, “Allah seized the kingdom of the Israelites on account of their mistreatment of the Prophets, verily the kingdom of this nation will also be seized by Allah on account of their hatred of ‘Ali b. Abi Talib”- Mizan al-I’tidal, Dhahabi v.2 p.251

What you’re about to see is something akin to Muslim chivalry: Dhulfiqar (holy doubled pointed sword of Imam Ali {as} given by

Mustafa Ahmad Muhammad ﷺ). These banners are woven during the 15th century and are often decorated with a two-bladed sword wielded by the Holy Prophet's ﷺ son-in-law 'Ali b. Abi Talib عَلَيْهِ ٱلسَّلَامُ and it's shield shaped. This particular banner, made in 1683 in North Africa, was made of metallic thread and maroon silk. Its inscription is written in the distinctive maghribi script with uniform thick letters and low sweeping curves.

"Allah, Allah, may our evenings be good; may good be unfolded to us; may evil be repelled from us; may our enemies and adversaries be subjugated; may the benevolent aid of the Twelve Imams be ever with us; may those among us who reach the goal be not severed from the train of the Twelve Imams; may they be shielded from slander; may our wishes be granted and our supplications accepted. This is the Rose Song (gülbang) of Muhammad: the light of the Prophet, the nobility of 'Alī; our pīr Muhammad Bahā ad-Dīn Uvaysī, present and watchful, outward and inward; HU, HU! (Allah Is, Allah Is!") [Risālat al-Tarīqat an-Naqshabandiya Aaliyah]

Without the previous "stuff" mentioned, we would fail miserably. "I" have taken the time to research and authenticate such "stuff" so that "I" may put it in this book for Baraka (Divine Blessings). May Allah Almighty accept this work from me, a weak and fragile slave of Allah Almighty. Again, any good you'll read within this book is from Allah Almighty, but any mistakes and badness you may read in this book Is certainly not from Allah Almighty, but from me, my own weaknesses and shortcomings. May Allah Almighty forgive us. Ameen! Ameen! Ameen!

وَمَنْ تَـكُنْ بِرَسُـولِ اللهِ نُصْرَتُـهُ

إِنْ تَلْقَهُ الْأُسْدُ فِي آجَـامِهَا تَجِمِ

Transliteration: Wa man takun bi rasooliLlaahi nusratuhu

-In talqahul -usdu fi aajaa mihaa tajimi!

Translation: The one who has the Messenger of Allah ﷺ as his aid and assistor then even if he were to go to the Lion's den, the lions would fear him! (Al Burdah Sharif, a section from chapter 8)

The power of this particular spiritual praising for **Mustafa Ahmad Muhammad** ﷺ is such that it protected Shaykh Nimar al-Khatib قدس الله سره from the bullets that were being shot at the car that he قدس الله سره was in. Hayy Mashallah! Sadly everyone else passed away, but he didn't, although his قدس الله سره shirt was pierced with bullets, his قدس الله سره skin wasn't. Hayy Mashallah! The Shaykh قدس الله سره said that the reason for that was that he قدس الله سره used to recite this praising upon **Mustafa Ahmad Muhammad** ﷺ every morning. Hayy Mashallah! So let us recite and become lions for Haqq, Divine Truth.

Na'lain Sharif (blessed sandal)
of **Mustafa Ahmad Muhammad** ﷺ.

201 NAMES OF MUSTAFA AHMAD MUHAMMAD ﷺ

1.	Mu*h*ammad	Most Praised One
2.	A*h*mad	Most Praiseworthy
3.	*H*âmid	One who praises Allâh
4.	Ma*h*mûd	Praised by all, Laudable
5.	A*h*yad	Protector of believers from hell-fire
6.	Wa*h*îd	Unique
7.	Mâ*h*î	Obliterator of disbelief
8.	*H*âshir	Summoner, Gatherer on the Day of Judgement
9.	‘Âqib	Successor of all the Prophets
10.	*T*âhâ	Tâhâ
11.	Yâsîn	Yâsîn
12.	*T*âhir	Pure, Clean
13.	Mu*t*ahhar	One purified by Allâh
14.	*T*ayyib	Good, Pleasant
15.	Sayyîd	Master of all
16.	Rasûl	The Messenger of Allâh

17.	Nabiyy	Prophet
18.	Rasûl u'r ra*h*mah	The Messenger of mercy
19.	Qayyim	Right and True, Straight
20.	Jâmi'	One who gathers in himself all perfections
21.	Muqtafî	One who succeeds all the Prophets
22.	Muqaffâ	One who is followed
23.	Rasûl u'l malâ*h*im	The Messenger of fierce battles against oppressive disbelievers
24.	Rasûl u'r râ*h*ah	The Messenger of comfort/ peaceful repose
25.	Kâmil	Perfect
26.	Iklîl	Crown
27.	Muddaththir	One Enveloped in a cloak/mantle
28.	Muzzammil	One Wrapped up in a garment
29.	'Abdullâh	Allâh's Ultimate Devotee
30.	*H*abîbullâh	The Beloved of Allâh
31.	Safiyyullâh	The Chosen One of Allâh
32.	Najiyyullâh	One in whom Allâh confides spiritual secrets
33.	Kalîmullâh	One who talks with Allâh
34.	Khâtim u'l Anbiyâ'	The Seal of the Prophets
35.	Khâtim u'r Rusul	The Seal of the Messengers

36.	Mu*h*yî	Vivifier of dead hearts with the light of faith
37.	Munjî	Leader to salvation
38.	Mudhakkir	One who reminds us of Allâh, Admonisher
39.	Nâsir	Helper
40.	Man*s*ûr	Helped by Allâh, Victorious
41.	Nabiyy u'r ra*h*mah	The Prophet of mercy
42.	Nabiyy u't tawbah	The Prophet of repentance
43.	Harî*s*un 'alaykum	Full of concern for you
44.	Ma'lûm	Well-known
45.	Shahîr	Celebrated, Famous
46.	Shâhid	Beholder
47.	Shahîd	Witness, Martyr
48.	Mashhûd	Witnessed, The Attested One
49.	Bashîr	Bearer of good news
50.	Mubashshir	Conveyor of glad tidings
51.	Nadhîr	Warner
52.	Mundhir	Warner, Dissuader from sin
53.	Nûr	Sacred light
54.	Sirâj	The Sun of Prophethood
55.	Misbâh	Luminous Lamp
56.	Hudâ	Right guidance

57.	Mahdi	Rightly guided
58.	Munîr	Illuminator
59.	Dâ'î	Inviter to Islâm
60.	Mad'uww	One called by Allâh
61.	Mujîb	Responsive
62.	Mujâb	One whose prayers/calls are answered
63.	*Hafiy*	Welcoming, Hospitable, Well-informed
64.	'Afuww	Pardoner
65.	Waliyy	Friend of Allâh, Friend of believers
66.	*H*aqq	Truth
67.	Qawiyy	Strong, Powerful
68.	Amîn	Trustworthy
69.	Ma'mûn	Trusted
70.	Karîm	Generous, Noble
71.	Mukarram	The ennobled one, Honoured, Venerable
72.	Makîn	Firm, Unshakeable
73.	Matîn	Firm, Authoritative
74.	Mubîn	Clear, Evident
75.	Mu'ammil	Hopeful
76.	Wa*s*ûl	Uniter
77.	Dhû quwwah	Possessor of power

78.	Dhû *h*urmah	Possessor of sacredness
79.	Dhû makânah	Possessor of firmly established high position
80.	Dhû 'izz	Possessor of might/honour
81.	Dhû Fa*d*l	Possessor of Allâh's grace/ bounty
82.	Mu*t*â'	One who is obeyed
83.	Mu*t*î'	One obedient to Allâh
84.	Qadamu *s*idq	One with a sincere footing
85.	Ra*h*mah	Mercy, Compassion
86.	Bushrâ	Glad tidings
87.	Ghawth	Saviour, Succour
88	Ghayth	Rain of mercy, brings dead hearts to life
89.	Ghiyâth	Helper, Saviour
90.	Ni'matullâh	Favour of Allâh
91.	Hadiyyatullâh	The Gift of Allâh
92.	'Urwatun wuthqâ	The Firm Tie that binds man to Allâh
93.	Sirâ*t*ullâh	The Path leading to Allâh
94.	Sirâ*t*un mustaqîm	The Straight Path
95.	Dhikrullâh	Personification of the remembrance of Allâh
96.	Sayfullâh	The sword of Allâh
97.	*H*izbullâh	Allâh's partisan

98.	An-Najm u'th-thâqib	The Piercing Star
99.	Mu*st*afâ	Divinely selected
100.	Mujtabâ	The Chosen One
101.	Muntaqâ	Chosen for his purity
102.	Ummi	Not taught by a human but directly by Allâh
103.	Mukhtâr	The Chosen One
104.	Ajîr	One who selflessly labours for Allâh, rewarded by Allâh
105.	Jabbâr	Compeller
106.	Abu'l Qâsim	The father of Qâsim
107.	Abu'*t T*âhir	The father of the Pure ('Abdullâh)
108.	Abu'*t T*ayyib	The father of the Pleasant ('Abdullâh)
109.	Abû Ibrâhîm	The father of Ibrâhîm
110.	Mushaffa'	The Accepted Intercessor
111.	Shafiy'	Intercessor
112.	Sâlih	Righteous, Virtuous, Pious, Devout
113.	Musli*h*	Conciliator, Peacemaker, Upright
114.	Muhaymin	Protector, Guardian
115.	Sâdiq	Truthful
116.	Musaddiq	One proved true, Confirmer, Verifier
117.	Sidq	Truthfulness, Sincerity
118.	Sayyid u'l Mursalîn	Master of all the Messengers of Allâh

119.	Imâm u'l muttaqîn	Leader of the pious who fear Allâh
120.	Qâ'id u'l ghurr i'l mu*h*ajjalîn	Leader of those with shining faces and limbs
121.	Khalîl u'r Ra*h*mân	The Friend of The Merciful Allâh
122.	Barr	Righteous, Pious
123.	Mabarr	Essence of piety
124.	Wajîh	Honourable, Illustrious
125.	Nasî*h*	Sincere Advisor
126.	Nâsi*h*	True Counsellor
127.	Wakîl	Faithful Trustee
128.	Mutawwakil	One who puts all his trust in Allâh
129.	Kafîl	Guarantor, Surety
130.	Shafîq	Compassionate, Kind
131.	Muqîm u's Sunnah	Establisher of the Sunnah
132.	Muqaddas	Sanctified one
133.	Rû*h* u'l qudus	Spirit of purity
134.	Rû*h* u'l haqq	Spirit of truth
135.	Rû*h* u'l qi*st*	Spirit of justice
136.	Kâfî	One who suffices here and in the Hereafter
137.	Muktafî	Contented (with little)
138.	Bâligh	One who has attained spiritual perfection

139.	Muballigh	The Deliverer of Allâh's Revelations
140.	Shâfî	Healer
141.	Wâsil	The one who completed his journey to Allâh
142.	Mawsûl	One bound by Allâh
143.	Sâbiq	First and foremost
144.	Sâ'iq	Leading/driving force, One who urges on
145.	Hâdî	Guide
146.	Muhdî	One who gives guidance
147.	Muqaddam	First and foremost, in the forefront
148.	'Azîz	Mighty, Honourable
149.	Fâ*d*il	Most Outstanding, Virtuous
150.	Mufa*dd*al	The Favoured One of Allâh
151.	Fâti*h*	Victorious, Opener of the doors of mercy
152.	Miftâ*h*	The Key
153.	Miftâ*h* u'r ra*h*mah	The Key to Allâh's mercy
154.	Miftâ*h* u'l jannah	The Key to paradise
155.	'Alam u'l îmân	Symbol of faith
156.	'Alam u'l yaqîn	Symbol of certitude
157.	Dalîl u'l khayrât	Guide to good deeds
158.	Musa*hh*ih u'l *h*asanât	Perfecter of good deeds

159.	Muqîl u'l 'atharât	Helper of those who stumble
160	*S*afû*h*un aniz zallât	Forgiver of offences
161.	*S*a*h*îb u'sh shafâ'ah	One endowed with intercession
162.	*S*â*h*ib u'l maqâm	Possessor of the highest rank/position
163.	*S*â*h*ib u'l qadam	One endued with precedence/lofty rank
164.	Makh*s*û*s* bi'l 'izz	Distinguished with exclusively special might/honour
165.	Makh*s*û*s* bi'l majd	Distinguished with exclusively special glory
166.	Makh*s*û*s* bi'sh sharaf	Distinguished with exclusively special nobility
167.	*S*â*h*ib u'l wasîlah	Possessor of the means to Allâh's Mercy
168.	*S*â*h*ib u's sayf	Owner of the sword against Allâh's enemies
169.	*S*â*h*îb u'l Fa*d*îlah	Possessor of Allâh's Grace
170.	*S*â*h*ib u'l izâr	Owner of the wrapper/ covering of prophethood
171.	*S*â*h*ib u'l *h*ujjah	Possessor of the proof
172.	*S*â*h*ib u's sul*t*ân	Owner of dominion/authority
173.	*S*â*h*ib u'r ridâ'	Owner of the covering cloth
174.	*S*â*h*ib u'd darajat i'r rafiy'ah	One endowed with the exalted position/rank
175.	*S*â*h*ib u't tâj	The Crowned One on the night of mi'râj

176.	*S*â*h*ib u'l mighfar	One who wears the helmet
177.	*S*â*h*ib u'l liwâ'	Holder of the banner
178.	*S*â*h*ib u'l mi'râj	Master of heavenly ascension
179.	*S*â*h*ib u'l qa*d*îb	Holder of the rod/staff
180	*S*â*h*ib u'l Burâq	The rider of the Burâq
181.	*S*â*h*ib u'l khâtam	Possessor of the Seal of Prophethood
182.	*S*â*h*ib u'l 'alâmah	Possessor of the Sign of Prophethood
183.	*S*â*h*ib u'l burhan	One endowed with the clear proof
184.	*S*â*h*ib u'l bayân	The Possessor of the Qur'ân
185.	Fasî*h* u'l lisân	Eloquent and effective of speech
186.	Mutahhar u'l janân	One with a purified heart who purifies hearts
187.	Raûf	Clement, Most Kind
188.	Ra*h*îm	Merciful
189.	Udhunu khayr	Hearer of good
190.	Sa*h*î*h* u'l Islâm	Establisher of the correct Message of Islâm
191.	Sayyid u'l kawnayn	Master of this world and the Hereafter
192.	'Ayn u'n na'îm	Source of Allâh's Blessings
193.	'Ayn u'l ghurr	Source of beauty/radiance
194.	Sa'dullâh	Joy of Allâh
195.	Sa'd u'l khalq	Joy of all creation
196.	Kha*t*îb u'l umam	Preacher to all humanity

197.	‘Alam u’l hudâ	The Sign of the guidance
198.	Kâshif u’l kurab	Remover of hardships/distress
199.	Râfi ‘u’r rutab	Raiser of the ranks of believers
200.	‘Izz u’l ‘Arab	Honour of the Arabs
201.	*S*â*h*ib u’l faraj	Source of bliss/comfort

TAHIAT AL-HABIB SALAWAT

Lover's Salutation

By Saqibi Seif

بِسْمِ اللهِ الرَّحْمٰنِ الرَّحِيْمِ

Transliteration: bismillāhi r-raḥmāni r-raḥīm

Translation: In the Name of Allah, the most Merciful, the most Compassionate

يا الله أبعث السلام والبركات على المختار وعلى أسرته المقدسة نيابة عن الحب الذي تحب لنفسك، والحب الذي يحبونه لك، وحبك

لنفسك

Transliteration: "Ya Allah 'ubeath alsalam walbarakat ealaa almukhtar waealaa 'usratih almuqadasat niabat ean alhabi aldhy tahibuh linafsika, walhabi aldhy yuhibuwnah laka, wahbak linafsik."

Translation:

"O God, send peace and blessings to the Chosen One and his holy family on behalf of the love You love for Yourself, the love they love for You, and Your love for Yourself." Ameen! Ameen! Ameen!

Benefit of This Salawat

This is a very powerful Salawat as it encompasses the essence of Haqq (Divine Truth) which cumulates from the Ahlul Bayt, from **Mustafa Ahmad Muhammad** ﷺ, and from Allah Almighty. Hayy Mashallah! Islam Is not Islam without the Ahlul Bayt and without **Mustafa Ahmad Muhammad** ﷺ, and so this Salawat contains the Islam that Allah Almighty intended for us to enjoy and call others to enjoin in it too.

Hayy Mashallah! This Salawat Is also endless in its rewards and blessings, for ALLAH ALMIGHTY Is sending Salawats upon the HAQQ on behalf of the LOVE HE HAS FOR HIMSELF, which is what? It cannot be described and on top of that, it Is such a Salawat that Is expressing the love that **Mustafa Ahmad Muhammad** ﷺ, Ahlul Bayt, and Allah Almighty love. Which is what? It cannot be described. This Salawat Is the love's love. The essence of our worship to Allah Almighty and love towards the Haqq and thus it's the Haqq's Haqq. Hayy Mashallah! Divine secrets are revealed to the one that recites this Salawat, as it Is for all Salawats, but this one Is the essence of the love that Salawats contain, and so it can be said that this Salawat Is the Essence of Benefit, which could be another name for this Salawat.

Al-Fatiha.

THE MUHAMMADAN SIPS FROM THE ETERNAL FOUNTAIN OF DIVINE LOVE

Sip 1

O my beloved one ﷺ, when "I" am your beloved, you are no more
my beloved, for this "I" is no more, and all
that Is, Is you, the "object" of all belovedness.
Look at what your love has made be say, it makes
me say crazy things! But this craziness for
you is the sign of real love and devotion
to you, "I", the beloved: Divine love ﷻ.

Sip 2

No matter the pain, the path of Ayn –(ع)–the Path of Ali عَلَيْهِ ٱلسَّلَامُ *- tears the world apart, from this pain it teases the gaze of The One without son, from Him showing the sun of love:* ***Mustafa Ahmad Muhammad*** ﷺ, *"I" then having gained a Heavenly gain to make me go so insane that sanity becomes my insanity and insanity being my sanity, sailing upon the seas of mercy, rowing my boat of Ishq (Mad Divine Love) as the rays from the sun shines upon "I", riding the waves of rapture, my ego telling me to capture her (the soul), but my soul goes "no", and "I" comply,*
becoming a slave to my soul's "no",
the Muhammadan Way ﷺ.

Sip 3

*With every gust of wind, tapping of the fingers on your desk when bored, the footsteps of every HU-man, "I" hear the beloved (**Mustafa Ahmad Muhammad** ﷺ) sing a song of heavenly magnitude which knows no end to its most beautiful lyrics and melodies–this is the essence ofthe state of the lover of Allah Almighty's most beloved one,*
***Mustafa Ahmad Muhammad** ﷺ!*

Sip 4

No one knows the extent and depth of love "I" have for you, ***O Mustafa Ahmad Muhammad*** ﷺ *, and thus no one knows the extent and depth of love you have for me,* ***O Mustafa Ahmad Muhammad*** ﷺ*!*

Sip 5

Your sandals, ***O Mustafa Ahmad Muhammad*** ﷺ*, the most beloved one of Allah Almighty, are my Heavens and the dust under your sandals are my countless earths where my spirit roams therein, guiding like-minded Individuals to you,* ***O Mustafa Ahmad Muhammad*** ﷺ*, echoing the Kun (Beingness) from Allah Almighty, the Hu of all existence, yet unbound by existence.*

Sip 6

"I" try to be worthy of your glance, ***O Mustafa Ahmad Muhammad*** *ﷺ, which Is an impossible challenge like trying to pick up a snowy mountain with blue grass with the tip of my small finger. But "I" try anyway, for your love Is so immense that in any way, neither here nor there, will tear apart the mountain, making it smaller than the blade of the blue grass that "I've" started with and heavier than the mountain, but somehow it Is also the lightest.*

Sip 7

Know that your love ***Mustafa Ahmad Muhammad*** ﷺ *Is the same as feeling the love that* ***Mustafa Ahmad Muhammad*** ﷺ *has for you, O HU-man, there Is no separation! Feel the ignorance of your "knowingness" and therefore being to feel the real knowingness that descends into the heart of Allah Almighty's most beloved one:* ***Mustafa Ahmad Muhammad*** ﷺ, ***O Mustafa Ahmad Muhammad*** ﷺ *help us with the words (mercies) from the "tongue" of Allah Almighty! And then if Allah Almighty wishes we will become a light from saints, the Divine lovers, peace and blessings be upon them all, if those words reach our hearts.*

Sip 8

My pain Is too much, ***O Mustafa Ahmad Muhammad*** *ﷺ, too much that it makes blasphemy my cure, blasphemy in your love, loving you,* ***O Mustafa Ahmad Muhammad*** *ﷺ more than "I" love myself and everyone in existence other than* ***you*** *ﷺ. Such a blasphemy Is so that "I" may make one of* ***your*** *ﷺ hadiths (sayings of* ***Mustafa Ahmad Muhammad*** *ﷺ) true, the hadith that says, "remember Allah so much that people call you mad", yes, "I" am a blasphemer, a mad one, mad in love for you ﷺ,* ***O Mustafa Ahmad Muhammad*** *ﷺ, loving you ﷺ is the best way to remember Allah Almighty, and if my love for you be wrong,* ***O Mustafa Ahmad Muhammad*** *ﷺ, at least it Is an honest offering from a weak slave like me, so let it Be on behalf of Allah Almighty's limitless mercy: let it Be, let it Be, let it Be...*

Sip 9

To me, there is only me, and thus to you, ***O Mustafa Ahmad Muhammad*** *ﷺ, there's only you ﷺ, containing all that wish to Be. "I" am, but you,* ***O Mustafa Ahmad Muhammad*** *ﷺ? Beyond the "I", for your love for Him is unmatched, and thus you ﷺ are incomprehensibly drenched in His mercy, a mercy that can only be tasted if there Is no "I", so "I" choose to be you ﷺ by trying to follow your way,* ***O Mustafa Ahmad Muhammad*** *ﷺ, so that "I" may taste His love, and your closeness to such a love,* ***O Mustafa Ahmad Muhammad*** *ﷺ, but "I" cannot, for you are you ﷺ and "I" am "I", and peace and blessings be upon your family, companions, holy lineage, slaves, lovers, and nation. Ameen! Ameen! Ameen!*

Sip 10

Loving you, ***O Mustafa Ahmad Muhammad*** ﷺ *Is more painful than the fire of hell and more pleasurable than heaven. How can this Be?* ***Your presence*** ﷺ *alone has enlightened my heart, cooled my eyes, and so "I'm" seeing things without logic, which thus shows me the secret of the soul.*

Sip 11

O Mustafa Ahmad Muhammad ﷺ*, I beg you to love me,* ***O Chosen One*** ﷺ*! So that The Oneness you're accepted by may choose "me" to Be in your love, free to Be "me"* ***(you*** ﷺ*) without hesitation.*

Sip 12

O Mustafa Ahmad Muhammad ﷺ*, my love for you causes me great discomfort. Is this pain you coming nearer to me or me getting further from* ***you*** ﷺ*? "I" must know before all that Is known comes to an "end" in my illusionary mind along with my never ending love to give to you,* ***O Mustafa Ahmad Muhammad*** ﷺ*!*

Sip 13

The whole world is turning for your love, ***O Mustafa Ahmad Muhammad*** *ﷺ, whereas "I" sit still in my handicapped state, burnt by this love that you contain in your being,* ***O the most perfected one*** *in Divinely Presence,* ***O Mustafa Ahmad Muhammad*** *ﷺ!*

Sip 14

Loving you ***Mustafa Ahmad Muhammad*** ﷺ *is making me scandalous and a sinful lover, but isn't that the point, to lose one's mind for* ***your*** ﷺ *eternal mind? To see nothing but* ***you*** ﷺ*, your love? This is the point of all points, like the dot under the Baa (second Arabic letter), being under the gaze of Ali* عَلَيْهِ ٱلسَّلَامُ *who/Hu Is the dot under the Baa.*

Sip 15

"I" try to speak of Him, losing "myself" in you
Mustafa Ahmad Muhammad ﷺ*; the Hu (Is-ness),*
and thus "I" am the Hu He mentions, for Hu
Is neither apart of ***you*** ﷺ *nor "me", but*
rather the part of Hu in wholeness Is in
you ﷺ*, apart of "me", therefore a*
*part of "I"...****you*** ﷺ*!*

Sip 16

My love for you ***Mustafa Ahmad Muhammad*** ﷺ *Is like the rain to the soil and the soil to the rain. Separated yet one in purpose, however the rain Is the rain (****you*** ﷺ*) and the soil ("I") is the soil.*

Sip 17

Nothing remains but the shine of ***your*** ﷺ *light when "I" am infused with your love,* ***O Mustafa Ahmad Muhammad*** ﷺ*, becoming one of the fabrics (Realities) of The Cloak (the Ahl al Bayt {holy household} of* ***Mustafa Ahmad Muhammad*** ﷺ*, peace and blessings be upon them all) that covers the entire universe, its cosmos, and beyond. This Is a Divine Secret that only* ***your*** ﷺ *lovers may know, taste, and experience this Heavenly Love, Knowledge, Wisdom, and thus Knowingness from our kind Allah Almighty.*

Sip 18

What shall "I" say to witness your beautiful face, ***O Mustafa Ahmad Muhammad*** ﷺ*? Shall "I" Say the name of Ali* عَلَيْهِ ٱلسَّلَامُ*? YA ALI (AS)! YA ALI (AS)! YA ALI (AS)! What shall "I" say to witness your most radiant face,* ***O Mustafa Ahmad Muhammad*** ﷺ*? Shall "I" say the name of Hussain* عَلَيْهِ ٱلسَّلَامُ*? YA HUSSAIN (AS)! YA HUSSAIN (AS)! YA HUSSAIN (AS)! What shall "I" say to witness your Divine Beauty,* ***O Mustafa Ahmad Muhammad*** ﷺ*? Shall "I" say Fatima* عَلَيْهِ ٱلسَّلَامُ*? YA FATIMA (AS)! YA FATIMA (AS)! YA FATIMA (AS)! What shall "I" say to have one glimpse of your Heavenly Grandeur,* ***O Mustafa Ahmad Muhammad*** ﷺ*? Shall I say Hassan* عَلَيْهِ ٱلسَّلَامُ*? YA HASSAN (AS)! YA HASSAN (AS)! YA HASSAN (AS)! What shall "I" say to have your approval,* ***O Mustafa Ahmad Muhammad*** ﷺ*? Shall "I" say Zainab* عَلَيْهِ ٱلسَّلَامُ*? YA ZAINAB (AS)! YA ZAINAB (AS)! YA ZAINAB (AS)! YA ZAINAB (AS)! What shall "I" say* ***O Mustafa Ahmad Muhammad*** ﷺ *so that "I" may see* ***you*** ﷺ*? We shouldn't despair in your mercy upon us, but "I" can't help but admit that every second that passes me by without having seen you* ﷺ *is like a hot knife digging deeper into my heart with every fleeting second,* ***O Mustafa Ahmad Muhammad*** ﷺ*! What shall "I" say? "I'm" nothing but a weak servant of Allah Almighty. Shall "I" say Allah Almighty? YA ALLAH ALMIGHTY! YA ALLAH ALMIGHTY! YA ALLAH ALMIGHTY! The tears of yearning from my eyes have dried up all in front of me as icy oceans. "I've" been cooked raw for your love,* ***O Mustafa Ahmad Muhammad*** ﷺ*. What shall "I" say* ***O Mustafa Ahmad Muhammad*** ﷺ*? What shall "I" say? What shall "I" say? What shall "I" say?...*

Sip 19

*The moon of light (**Mustafa Ahmad Muhammad** ﷺ) was born in the hour of darkness and then the hour of darkness became a sun of light. Anyone with an open heart that gazed upon the moon's light became one of the sun's ray and anyone with an open heart that gazed upon the sun became one of the lights from the moon's delight: **Mustafa Ahmad Muhammad** ﷺ!*

Sip 20

O Green Falcon, Imam Mahdi عَلَيْهِ ٱلسَّلَامُ, "I" am waiting for your arrival in the skies (haqiqahs {Divine Realities}) of Divine Truth (Haqq). ***O Mustafa Ahmad Muhammad*** *ﷺ, we have lost sight of your holy Proof of the Green Falcon (as), we're making truce with satan! O the Shine of all existence ﷺ;* ***Mustafa Ahmad Muhammad*** *ﷺ, your Presence leaves me dumbfounded, unarmed to feel every stab of your ﷺ sword of love. This Way has begun a death in me that "I" may never escape from and a life that will always resurrect me into the embrace of Your Grace, O Allah Almighty! Allow this lowly slave of Yours to be embraced in Your lights and dignity so that Your light may shine through "I", gifting me the sight of the Green Falcon (as) in the skies of Truth forever more.*

Sip 21

If "I'm" blasphemous, Allah Almighty's love made me do it. If "I" act like an atheist, my annihilation in Allah Almighty made me do it. If "I" say and do whatever "I" like, Allah Almighty's warm embrace made me do it. Hayy Mashallah! Call me whatever you like, for its title has already been bestowed upon me by Allah Almighty, from Allah Almighty, "for" Allah Almighty, but not of Allah Almighty. If "I" go into a mosque with a cross and a bible and if "I" go into a church with a tasbih (rosary) and the holy Qur'an, with the love of ***Mustafa Ahmad Muhammad*** ﷺ *in my heart, Allah Almighty's Compassion and Unity made me do it. If "I" hang around the lowly and deprived, Allah Almighty's bounties made me do it. If "I" give up my faith, Allah Almighty's unveiling made me do it. If "I" hold onto my faith, Allah Almighty's signs firmly hold a place in my path towards Haqq, Divine Truth. If "I" kiss the beautiful, fragrant, and blessed soles of* ***Mustafa Ahmad Muhammad*** ﷺ, *more than the black stone on the Ka'aba, my intoxicated love for him,* ***Mustafa Ahmad Muhammad*** ﷺ, *made me do it, and thus "I've" succeeded in my Islam.*

Sip 22

The School of Love Is the Love itself, its classroom Is hidden in plain sight, and thus many are blind to it, they think (that's the problem) that it Is something tangible, that "If I get something, then Love will be presented to me in the best of forms." But Love has no form, form Is lust, it Is beyond lust where Love makes itself known, through the hidden, and only the people who/Hu are silent/still enough will be able to not only see the hidden Love, they too will become the hidden, covered, and shaded under the royal "garment" of mercy from Hu's Grace. Hayy Mashallah! When the student of Love gets enrolled into the class of no abode, consider him/her truly alive, having been guided through death. Dying before dying, truly becoming alive. Such a student will be so high on such a Divine ecstasy upon tasting the sacred wine of Hu's command, so high that for him/her spiritual states will Be like pebbles, it will come onto his/her lap in vast amounts, sharing them to whomever desires it, sincerely, making no distinction between race nor tradition, leaving nothing for himself/herself, the only way to get more is to be empty, and therefore being under the most blessed feet of the most beloved and holy one, Mustafa Amhad Muhammad ﷺ! Such a love holds infinite remnants of the Lover's soul scattered all over the globe and beyond, for the Love in whole will obliterate us. This treasure of inner beauty Is found wherever your face turns if one Is sincere and humble. Know that the reflection sees its reflection not as a reflection, but as the self of its mirrored view. Deluded and awakened simultaneously. Absorbed in the dance that Allah Almighty has ordered creation to dance to: Love. Loving ***Mustafa Ahmad Muhammad*** *ﷺ!*

Sip 23

"I" was once looking for my soul and my soul was looking for "I", not knowing that my Soul Is the reflection of "I" and "I" the reflection of Soul (The Muhammadan Reality) that this Is nothing but the embrace of

"Self" love, for the only Soul to truly exist Is the Soul of ***Mustafa Ahmad Muhammad*** ﷺ *and it Is this empowerment of "self" which empowers the darkness into light and light into more light. When one truly embraces the "self", then that one begins to annihilate oneself into light upon light and upon light; the essence of the mystic, the treasure of the spiritual traveller, and the ruby lips of the most beloved one,* ***Mustafa Ahmad Muhammad*** ﷺ*!*

Sip 24

What "I've" learnt from these sips of Divine Love Is that love Is like a fussy child, it wants to hug you, but also it wants to be left alone. The love for ***Mustafa Ahmad Muhammad*** ﷺ *Is so delicate that it Is the most destructive thing there Is, if not taken care of. This love has highs and "lows" like that of a fussy child, but it purifies us. Hayy Mashallah!*

Sip 25

"I" (my impure ego) has lost all reason to live and yet "I" still yearn for a life worth living. Divine yearning, the yearning for the love of ***Mustafa Ahmad Muhammad*** ﷺ *does that to you.*

Sip 26

My only aim/wish Is to Be a sword for the Awliya (friends/saints of Allah Almighty, peace and blessings be upon them all), but if "I" can't be a sword for them, then at least its handle, and if not the handle, then at least the shadow that follows their sword, and if not the shadow, than at least the dust that's flying into the air from the land of Haqq (Divine Truth) through the swing of their blessed Divinely sword of Truth, but even if "I" cannot be that, then "I'd" love to Be at least a fleeting thought within their sacred minds, for that means "I" am with them, and they are with me. Hayy Mashallah! That would be a Divine Love story unheard, only felt within the Qalb (Heart) of ***Mustafa Ahmad Muhammad*** ﷺ*, for there are no words to describe/express such a heavenly beauty, for any word/expression used to carry it will be crushed by the heavenly weight of the Divinely Love that is forever eternal, never to be described/expressed through the 3D world of limitations, forms, and illusions. If "I" still cannot be all that, I'd love to be my yearning for them in my heart, for then "I'm" always occupied with them, and them with me, internally. But if "I" also cannot be that, that Is okay, for they have forgotten me, "I" have forgotten them, the will of Allah Almighty, whatever it Is, prevails over all, and "I" should be happy with the will of Allah Almighty, for only then will the saints, peace and blessings be upon them all, be happy with me, and make me into their soldier of Truth, not only the fragmentations of what my impure ego desires, but what my soul already Is. Which is what? Only Allah Almighty knows, for "I" know not, for the "I" Is actually non-existent and therefore Allah Almighty Is the one asking for these things from His saints, peace and blessings be upon them all, and so "I" become the blade, the handle, the shadow, the dirt, the fleeting Divine thoughts, the friend of Allah Almighty fighting for Haqq, for there Is no "I", only* ***he, The Universal Soul of Mustafa Ahmad Muhammad*** ﷺ*...if only "I" could control my impure ego..."I" need to drink some more of this Divine wine for that to happen!*

Sip 27

O Mustafa Ahmad Muhammad ﷺ*, the most yearned one in the Divinely Presence, my tomorrow Is in the next moment, yearning for the past self that yearned for you,* ***O Mustafa Ahmad Muhammad*** ﷺ*...oh ever so pure it was, now "I'm" losing myself again, so that your Beauty may Be unveiling through me forever more, becoming lost again, so that "I" may be freshly found sane within the insanity of my love for your grandeur, the Divine kiss for all those who/Hu ponder,* ***O Mustafa Ahmad Muhammad*** ﷺ*! O yearning one (the soul of "I") this yearning itself Is the treasure you've been seeking for millennia, O soul, why not rest, put down the pen and paper and let go of the impure ego test, let the Divine contest on behalf of you, for this world Is for the one that's running after the worldly contesting for worldly riches. It Is He who/Hu expects you to fetch a spec of Divinity from the most beloved one,* ***Mustafa Ahmad Muhammad*** ﷺ *so the ache of our yearning is no more, all sores gone, back to where they came from/belong: nothingness. O you who/Hu yearns, you are the BISMILLAH (in the Name of Allah), every intention you hold is the INSHALLAH (If Allah Wills it), every step you take is the Kun Faya Kun Salah (Be & It Is Prayer), for He Is closer to us than our jugular vein, and thus your real worship has then found its preciousness. Enter the gate of Ali* عَلَيْهِ ٱلسَّلَامُ*, let him (as) behead your falsity of impure ego, and enter into the ocean of ecstasy, the spiritual states of his (as) Divine Victory, coming from* ***The Universal Soul of Mustafa Ahmad Muhammad*** ﷺ*! Hayy Mashallah!*

Sip 28

Divine Dreams they (Mustafa Ahdmad Muhammad ﷺ, the Ahl al Bayt, and companions, peace and blessings be upon them all), had yet we continue to assume what their hearts had seen, a Heavenly beauty that only suits He. They struggled for Truth so hard and got so far, beyond the par of saints, peace and blessings be upon them all, painting the land of Truth with their blood of sacred pain. Satan stumbling over his own filth, confused. Zainab عَلَيْهِ ٱلسَّلَامُ running left to right to defend what's right, as the warrior she Is, whizzing sharper than the wind on a stormy night, frightened by no one other than His might, a sight to behold, a Divine flight that we seekers try to Be and hold her (as) sacredness, but failing to do so, for nothing can match her (as) ail, for no one can match the pain of the Ahl al Bayt (holy house household of ***Mustafa Ahmad Muhammad*** *ﷺ, majestic peace and blessings be upon him, his family, companions, holy linage, slaves/lovers, and nation)– boarding the ship of Divine sacrifice, sailing upon the seas of Heavenly signs, of pain that Is forever near them, and so far from us, yet we have the audacity to complain of the life we live when they gave up their whole lives for Truth while we give nothing other than the something of our impure egos?! We are walking on thin ice, dancing and flirting with the devil, tap dancing with joy, oblivious to all that has happened to holy ones, peace and blessings be upon them all, an antichrist poly deployed by the enemies of righteousness, testing the purity of our hearts, turning it into viscousness, departing from holy grounds, shoved deep under the earth, reversed back to our homeland; either heaven or hell, depending on where we are spending our swell time with: Ahl al Bayt or the bait from satan? But know if this Is all fate, then we* *would not be gifted with freewill, and therefore piety Is nothing but a facade. Bloodline doesn't matter if you're on Haqq, Divine Truth, for Abu Lahab saw the crown of all existence (**Mustafa Ahmad Muhammad** ﷺ) and yet he still kneeled to satan, his freewill was so evil that his fate was forever sealed from the beginning. So if you're good, you're free, if you're bad, you're blind, lead by your inner devils down towards hell with no luxury to truly see with the Noor (Divine Light) of **Mustafa Ahmad Muhammad** ﷺ! Zainab عَلَيْهِ ٱلسَّلَامُ came with the cup of Heavenly delight as did the Ahl al Bayt, peace and blessings be upon them all, and the whole world tried to make them fold, but despite how hard they tried, Allah Almighty elevated them beyond comprehension, for they are the drops of wine that make **The Muhammadan Drink** ﷺ, they are the cup and cup bearers! Hayy Mashallah!*

Sip 29

Whenever you run towards goodness, then you are being dressed by the ***Muhammadan Reality*** *ﷺ, instantly, knowingly Muslim or not, as long as one Is sincere. Such a sacred reality Is not only exclusive to known Muslims, for that would put Allah Almighty's mercy at our level, which Is nothing unless Allah Almighty says it's something. May Allah Almighty forgive us! Know that all the wisdom and positive progression of HU-MAN-KIND Is from the Muhammadan Reality; the HU, Allah's Kun (Beingness), which Is what makes this world and many other infinite worlds to spin along with the infinite universes. When one Is entering into the ocean of goodness, the ocean of Mercy, Grace, then Love Is opened within that ocean, as far as the eye can see, and beyond that, beyond this too, forever more, never ending. To Be under the banner of the ummah (nation) of* ***Mustafa Ahmad Muhammad*** *ﷺ, majestic peace and blessings be upon him, his family, companions, holy lineage, slaves/lovers, and nation, one must be loyal to goodness, even if that means that goodness strips you away from all dignity and social standing, but you must try your utmost best to uphold goodness in a high regard, and when one Is doing such a thing, then he/she Is a Muslim, knowingly or not, for the Kalimah (Islamic declaration of faith) Is being recited by* ***The Ultimate Universal Soul of that one (Mustafa Ahmad Muhammad*** *ﷺ), and thus our minds and hearts become pure birds flying all over the globe to chirp songs of Divine beauty. Mercy. Compassion. Doing nothing but to respect the* ***Muhammadan Reality*** *ﷺ by respecting goodness, even if it's going against popular opinion, which Is what forms society as we know it, will earn us His good pleasure. It doesn't matter if a Muslim prays five times a day, if such a one fails in goodness, their prayers are most likely to be rejected.*

Sip 30

Giving Salawats (Salutations) to ***Mustafa Ahmad Muhammad*** ﷺ *Is not only in reciting it from the tongue, but it's also in reciting/feeling it from the heart. Without words, for how can we truly salute and praise the one that ALLAH ALMIGHTY Is already saluting and praising? Hayy Mashallah! This doesn't mean that we don't recite it from the tongue, for Allah Almighty loves for us to Be from the people of HUMBLENESS, for that Is the characteristic of* ***Mustafa Ahmad Muhammad****'s* ﷺ *ummah (nation). But how do we salute and praise* ***Mustafa Ahmad Muhammad*** ﷺ *from our hearts without words? You do and be good. Offer goodness to other people. Offer people ease and satisfaction, given that it's not going against Allah Almighty's Way. Hayy Mashallah! When we are embodying and providing goodness to people, we are saluting and praising the essence of* ***Mustafa Ahmad Muhammad*** ﷺ*, for he Is only bringing one thing to HU-MAN-KIND: goodness. Purity. Positivity. Glad tidings. Yes,* ***he*** ﷺ *made people AWARE of immorality and its dangers/horrors, but* ***he*** ﷺ *didn't embody nor bring immorality, for that's satan's job. Satan isn't offering and bringing mercy/goodness/pure ease, but rather he's bringing despair, arrogance, and all immorality that we can possibly imagine...beyond that too. Therefore when we are being bad, we are saluting and praising the reality of satan. May Allah Almighty forgive and protect us from that! However if we are being good, we are saluting and praising the reality of* ***Mustafa Ahmad Muhammad*** ﷺ*! Hayy Mashallah! May Allah Almighty always keep us in such a salutation and praising! When we're also sacrificing ourselves for the betterment of others, then we are also saluting and praising the reality of Ali* عَلَيْهِ ٱلسَّلَامُ*, of the Ahl al Bayt, the holy household of* ***Mustafa Ahmad Muhammad*** ﷺ*,peace and blessings be upon them all.*

Sip 31

Your love ***O Mustafa Ahmad Muhammad*** *ﷺ turns me into a disgraced one as well as a graceful one. Your love has made me feel as if I'm a scholar of supreme knowledge, but it has also caused me to be a beggar at every door, begging for knowledge. Your love has made me into a king and a slave, it has made me conscious and unconscious again and again without any sense of self. The more "I'm" in need, the more you snatch me closer to a secret embrace that none other than* ***your*** *ﷺ lovers may experience. This love has made me a hypocrite and a pious one. It has made me poor and rich, it has made me desirous and numb, it has made me neither here nor there - this love has made me see and taste the water as the wine and wine as the water. It has made me wild and tamed, forgetting my limits, Being with our Allah Almighty, The One who/Hu has not a name nor the name beneath the name - all these names are my spiritual states, my numbness and desires ever increase and decrease, embraced by You even more secretively until "I" die of "myself" so that all that's left Is Hu; Your creation of Beingness, to Be, Be, and Be some more, knowing no beginning nor ending to Your creation, To Your Love - Being One with all ancient stories that You have told within Yourself from Yourself and not of Yourself, revealing the Qur'an, the endless ocean of wine to the forever orignal cup bearer of that wine:* ***Mustafa Ahmad Muhammad*** *ﷺ! Anyone seeking this taste of Your Love becomes a Muhammadan, but what do You call the one who/Hu seeks the taste of Your taste, O The Most Unique One? I am lost in the cup and ocean of wine, now take me to Your chambers of an never ending secrecy so "I" may dance for Your Love in The Divinely Presence, for no one will Be able to understand this intoxication other than the lost ones in Your B(e)reath - our death (life).*

Sip 32

You don't have to wear everything green/the colour you want to wear to say that you're wearing green/the colour you want to wear. You just wear a little bit of green or whatever colour you want to wear and its reality of the colour Is not lessened due to the amount of it that you wear. Similarly, when you send one salutation/praising to ***Mustafa Ahmad Muhammad*** ﷺ *then you're from the people who/Hu send such salutations, you don't have to send countless salutations to* ***Mustafa Ahmad Muhammad*** ﷺ *to Be considered from such a Heavenly, blessed, and sacred group of HU-mans. But there's no harm in sending much salutations and praising to* ***Mustafa Ahmad Muhammad*** ﷺ*! The reality of sending one salutation and praising and sending much a salutation and praising are the same in regards to the spiritual lights that will dress your soul. Think of it this way: drawing a dot of any colour you want on a piece of paper and then colouring another page full of the colour you drew the dot with, the reality of the colour Is not diminished. It's still the colour that's expressed. So don't feel sad if you cannot do this much or that much in regards to the next person, for Allah Almighty gave everyone their spiritual provision according to the Divine Promise we made on the day of promises. Just Be sincere in whatever you're doing and you will never despair nor grieve. Understand that each pen carries its own colour and the pen to express that may differ from the next one, but it's still ink, it's still colour, it's still a pen. Each HU-man carries with them a spiritual pen, ink, and colour that's unique from HU-man to HU-man, this Is gifted by* ***Mustafa Ahmad Muhammad*** ﷺ *on the day of Divine Promises. We just need to find it. And whether a line or a dot Is drawn, it's not wrong, for all of it comes from the same source, and it depends on what you want to express which* *will require different shapes, inks, colours, and movements of the pen. When one draws negative things from the pen, then they have not paid their full respect to the one that gifted such a one with the pen. This pen Is intention and the colour Is your Sirr Al Sirr (Innermost Secret of Secrets).*

Sip 33

Allah Almighty Is saying that He doesn't mind being put into a form. Yes. In a Hadith Qudsi (Divine Tradition/Saying from Allah Almighty) it Is said that "I am whatever my servants think of me." Thoughts are a type of form, it's a form in which operates in your mind, in our life, and perception. This mind, thought, and ultimately perception perceives any world of form. It's either that or ALLAH ALMIGHTY IS WITHIN US, for Allah Almighty Is also saying that nothing could contain Him other than the heart of the believer. But that's still a form. So does Allah Almighty even exist? Is He even real? Yes. But not like how we've been indoctrinated to believe Him to Be. Form or no form. Material or immaterial. External or internal. It makes no difference, the HAQQ, DIVINE TRUTH, Is always One, it's always apparent regardless of where and how it appears as long as one Is sincere and pure. To Be sincere and pure all we must do Is dissolve the illusion that Is "I" and realise all there Is, Is Allah Almighty, and the one that's truly realising this Is ***The Universal Soul*** ﷺ*, "you" aren't realising/doing anything. The only real HU-man Is* ***Mustafa*** Ahmad Muhammad ﷺ *and so when we are being HU-mans and not animalistic, we are on the frequency from which ALLAH ALMIGHTY MADE THE LIGHT OF* ***MUSTAFA AHMAD MUHAMMAD*** ﷺ*, we then became droplets from his* ﷺ *endless Heavenly Light oceans, merging into them, effacing our identities, leaving no room for illusion of the "I", realising that all there Is, Is The Muhammadan Reality/Light that's always in limitless communication with Allah Almighty, and when* ***he*** ﷺ *Is in communication with Allah Almighty, then such endless oceans become like a huge electrical wave of lightening, moving through His QUDRA (POWER) Realities/Lights, cleansing, dressing, and* *blessing everything in existence! Giving anything and everything life. Whenever Allah Almighty wants to give someone/something life, He becomes apparent in the external, giving life colour, joy, and Heavenly tastes for us to devour in. He doesn't become apparent as HE IS, BUT IT'S THE THOUGHT/INTENTION WE HAVE OF HIM that appears through the filters of our inner colour, reviving us to Be who/Hu Allah Almighty has positively ordained for us, and this reviving Is* ***Mustafa Ahmad Muhammad****'s ﷺ b(e)reath. Hayy Mashallah!*

CONCLUDING THOUGHTS

"I" hope that these pages have invigorated your love for **Mustafa Ahmad Muhammad** ﷺ and that these pages have also made you understand the most unique taste of spirituality which Is The Muhammadan Drink, The Way of Sufism; the essence of Islam and all true religion, which Is Islam, for Islam Is the only true religion–the religions before the physical manifestation of **Mustafa Ahmad Muhammad** ﷺ were various aspects of Islam, various prophets, peace and blessings be upon them all, carried various Divine secrets (sips) from The Muhammadan Drink, and **Mustafa Ahmad Muhammad** ﷺ Is no sip, but rather he ﷺ Is forever the original Drink itself, and beyond without limitations, for Allah Almighty Is saluting and praising **Mustafa Ahmad Muhammad** ﷺ limitlessly. Hayy Mashallah!

وَمَنْ تَكُنْ بِرَسُولِ اللهِ نُصْرَتُهُ

إِنْ تَلْقَهُ الْأُسْدُ فِي آجَامِهَا تَجِمِ

Transliteration: Wa man takun bi rasooliLlaahi nusratuhu
-In talqahul -usdu fi aajaa mihaa tajimi

Translation: The one who has the Messenger of Allah ﷺ as his aid and assistor then even if he were to go to the Lion's den, the lions would fear him! (Al Burdah Sharif, a section from chapter 8)

SALAWATS UPON MUSTAFA AHMAD MUHAMMAD ﷺ + NADI ALI (AS)

بِسْمِ اللهِ الرَّحْمٰنِ الرَّحِيْمِ

Transliteration: bismillāhi r-raḥmāni r-raḥīm

Translation: In the Name of Allah, the most Merciful, the most Compassionate

Salawat Al-Fatih / The Salutation of the Victor

اَللّٰهُمَّ صَلِّ عَلى سَيِّدِنَا مُحَمَّدٍ اَلْفَاتِحِ لِمَا أُغْلِقَ وَ اَلْخَاتِمِ لِمَا سَبَقَ نَاصِرِ الْحَقِّ بِالْحَقِّ وَ الْهَادِي إلى صِرَاطِكَ الْمُسْتَقِيمِ وَ عَلَى آلِهِ حَقَّ قَدْرِهِ و مِقْدَارِهِ الْعَظِيم

"Allahumma salli `alaa Sayyidinaa Muhammadi 'l-faatihi limaa ughliq, wa 'l-khaatimi limaa sabaq, naasiri 'l-haqqi bi 'l-haqq, wa 'l-haadi ilaa Siraatika 'l-Mustaqeem, wa `alaa aalihi haqqa qadrihi wa miqdaarihi 'l-`azheem."

"O Allah, bless our Master Muhammad, who opened what was closed and sealed what was before. He makes the truth victorious by the truth and he is the guide to Your Straight Path. And bless his Household as it befits his immense stature and splendor." Ameen! Ameen! Ameen!

Scholars have said if you recite this once, it is as if you recited Dala`il al-Khayrat 600,000 times! Another says if you recite salawat on the number of human beings from the time of Sayyidina Adam (as) until Judgment Day, that is the value of Salaat al-Faatih!

Transliteration: "Allahuma salli ala Sayyinda Muhammadin adada hilmika wa salli ala Sayyinda Muhammadin adada ilmika wa salli ala Sayyidna Muhammadin adada kalimatika!" Ameen! Ameen! Ameen!

The Salawat above is from a section from the Dala'il al-Khayrat (The Waymarks of Benefits & Brilliant Burst of Lights in the Remembrance of Blessings on the Chosen Prophet), written by Muhammad Sulaiman al-Jazuli قدس الله سره.

Translation: "O Allah, exalt our Master Muhammad to the extent of Your Forbearance! O Allah, exalt our master Muhammad to the extent of Your Knowledge! O Allah, exalt our Master Muhammad on the number of Your Words!" Ameen! Ameen! Ameen!

NADI ALI (AS)

بِسۡمِ اللّٰهِ الرَّحۡمٰنِ الرَّحِيۡمِ

نَادِ عَلِيًّا مَظۡهَرَ الۡعَجَآئِبِ تَجِدۡهُ عَوۡنًا لَّكَ

فِى النَّوَآئِبِ كُلُّ هَمٍّ وَّغَمٍّ سَيَنۡجَلِىۡ

بِعَظَمَتِكَ يَآ اَللّٰهُ وَبِنُبُوَّتِكَ يَا مُحَمَّدُ

وَبِوَلَايَتِكَ يَا عَلِيُّ يَا عَلِيُّ يَا عَلِيُّ

Transliteration: bismillāhi r-raḥmāni r-raḥīm

Nadi Aliyan Madh'haral Ajaaeb
Tajid'hoo Aunnallaka Fin-Nawaaib
Kullu Hammin Wa Ghammin Sayanjali
Be Azmatika Ya Allah Hu
Be Nabooatika Ya Muhammadu
Be Wilaayatika Yaa Aliyyu, Yaa Aliyyu, Yaa Aliyu!

Translation: In the name of Allah, the most Merciful, the most Compassionate

Call upon Imam Ali عَلَيْهِ ٱلسَّلَامُ who manifests wondrous appearances, he will rescue and support you in times of difficulties and calamities. All grief and sorrows will disappear, By the Might of Allah, by Thy Apostleship! O Muhammad ﷺ, and by Thy Authority O Ali (as)! O Ali (as)! O Ali (as)!

بسم الله الرحمن الرحيم
لا اله الا الله محمد رسول الله صلى الله عليه وسلم
ولا حول ولا قوة الا بالله العلي العظيم

لا
إله
إلاالله
محمد
رَسُولُ
اللهُ

www.ingramcontent.com/pod-product-compliance
Lightning Source LLC
LaVergne TN
LVHW051019080826
845145LV00009B/2695

* 9 7 8 1 7 7 7 4 5 8 4 9 2 *